Program Guide

Cover Illustration: top Maurie Manning; bottom Amy Wummer.
Cover Photographs: (Solar System) JPL/NASA; (Snowboarder) ©Duomo/CORBIS; (Jaime Escalante) ©David Butow/CORBIS SABA.

Interior Photographs by Harcourt Achieve Collection ©2006 Harcourt Achieve Inc.

Rigby • Saxon • Steck-Vaughn

www.HarcourtAchieve.com
1.800.531.5015

Table of Contents

InStep Readers

Professional Handbook

Assessment

Appendix

> ▶ **SR**   content and instruction
>   specifically for
>   struggling readers
>
> ▶ **ELL**   content and instruction
>   specifically for English
>   language learners

RIGBY

in step
READERS

InStep Readers uses the only leveling system focused on the three key competencies of reading, language, and developmental phonics. With *Instep*, English language learners and struggling readers in grades 3–8 systematically and gradually improve toward on-grade-level reading proficiency and academic success!

Each level provides English language learners and struggling readers with progressive challenges and scaffolded instruction in **three key competencies**.

Three Key Competencies

▶ Reading Skills

New genres and features are gradually introduced across levels, allowing students to master the skills before moving to the next level.

▶ Developmental Phonics

Phonics skills are introduced in a research-proven sequence appropriate to each student's reading level.

▶ Language Skills

The introduction of new language structures is carefully controlled, enabling students to learn and succeed as they move up the levels.

Using InStep Readers

Step 1

Identify Reading Level

The Screener allows teachers to quickly and easily identify each student's reading level.

Step 2

Instruct

Five Student Readers and corresponding Teaching Booklets at each of 20 levels provide support in three key competencies and challenges to move students to the next reading level.

Step 3

Assess

Assessment Blackline Masters for each book allow teachers to assess mastery of the three key competencies taught.

Step 4

Achieve
On-Grade-Level Literacy

Students progress through each level, working toward on-grade-level literacy.

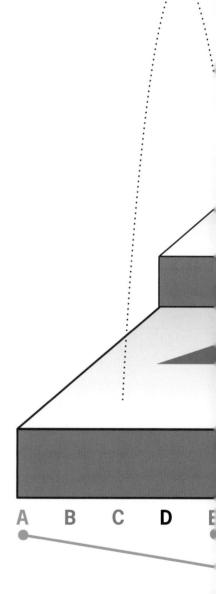

A   B   C   D   E

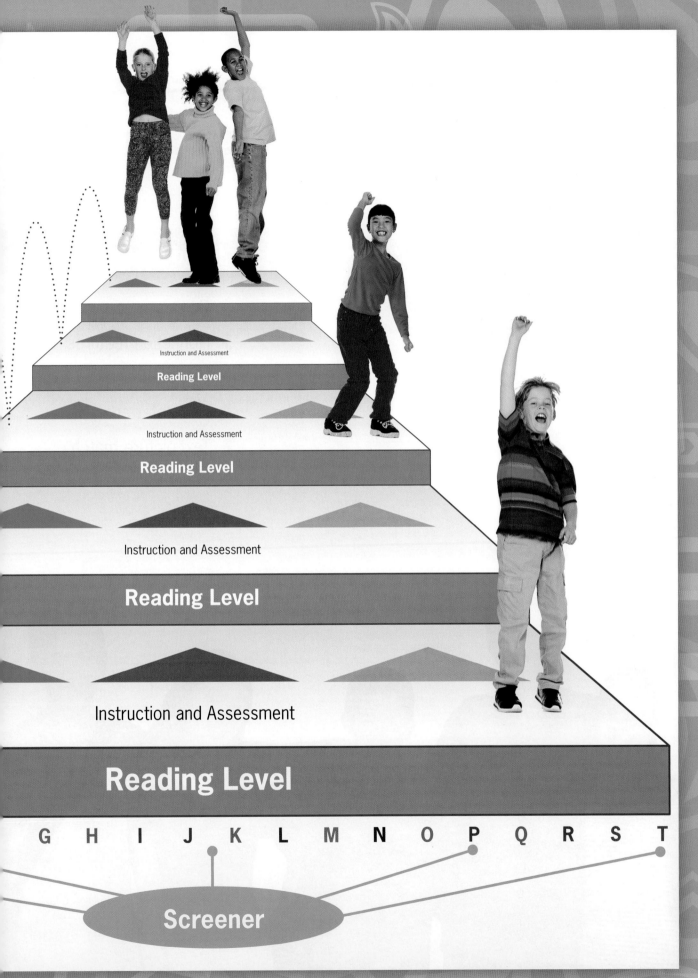

Instruction and Assessment

Reading Level

Instruction and Assessment

Reading Level

Instruction and Assessment

Reading Level

Instruction and Assessment

Reading Level

G H I J K L M N O P Q R S T

Screener

Instruct and Assess in Three Key Competencies

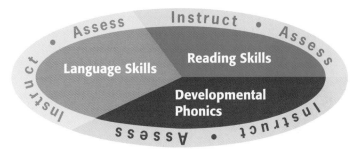

Reading Skills

▶ Genres

▶ Nonfiction features

▶ High-frequency words

▶ Character analysis

▶ Text-picture match

▶ Punctuation

Developmental Phonics

▶ Phonemic Awareness

▶ Consonants

▶ Short vowels

▶ Long vowels

▶ Consonant blends

▶ Digraphs

▶ Consonant patterns

▶ Vowel patterns

▶ Word-study skills

Language Skills

▶ Sentence structures (grammar)

▶ Literary constructions

▶ Multiple-meaning words and other language challenges

▶ High-utility words and concepts useful in school

See pages 10–11 for a detailed explanation of Developmental Phonics.

Teach the Right Phonics Skill at the Right Time!

Developmental Phonics means teaching the phonics skill appropriate to each student's level of literacy development.

Research-Based Sequence of Phonics Acquisition	
Phonemic Awareness	Including sound matching and sound segmenting ▶
Alphabet Knowledge	Including beginning consonants and short vowels ▶
Sound-Symbol Patterns	Including CVCe and other common and uncommon long-vowel patterns ▶
Meaning (Word Study)	Including prefixes and suffixes ▶

This chart is based on information provided in the following source:
Marcia Invernizzi and Latisha Hayes, University of Virginia, Charlottesville, VA
"Developmental-spelling research: A systematic imperative"
Reading Research Quarterly, vol. 39, no. 2 (International Reading Association).

Phonics instruction does not relate solely to age or to grade level—especially for English language learners and struggling readers.

Phonemic Awareness

Levels A–C: Sound matching, sound isolation, phoneme blending, segmentation, word and syllable awareness

Levels D–E: Adding and deleting sounds

Alphabet Knowledge

Level A: Beginning consonants

Levels B–E: short- and long-vowel word families

Sound-Symbol Patterns

Levels F–G: Consonant blends and digraphs

Level H: Common long-vowel patterns (digraphs)

Level I: Final blends

Level J: Complex consonant clusters

Level K: *r*-Controlled vowels, diphthongs

Level L: Uncommon vowel patterns

Level M: CVC*e* patterns

Meaning (Word Study)

Level N: Adjectives, verbs, prepositions, prefixes, contractions

Level O: Multiple-meaning words, adverbs, nouns, consonant doubling

Level P: Pronouns and conjunctions

Level Q: Connotation vs. denotation, analogies

Level R: Antonyms, open and closed syllables, inflected endings

Level S: Compound words

Level T: Homonyms

A Dual Path for Meeting Different Needs

	Build Background	Vocabulary
English Language Learners	Preview unfamiliar concepts.	Build a solid vocabulary foundation.
Struggling Readers	Motivate students.	Expand understanding of vocabulary.

Reading the Text	Response
Scaffold reading for beginning language learners with teacher support.	Activate vocabulary and concepts in prewriting.
Follow one clear lesson plan with all struggling readers.	Connect text to self.

Just 10 Minutes to Start a Student in a Reading Level

The Screener enables you to easily and quickly screen your students and start them at a reading level.

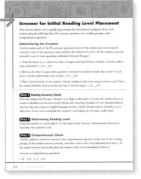

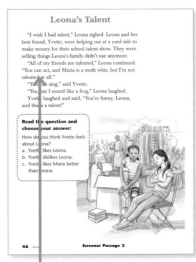

Leona's Talent

"I wish I had talent," Leona sighed. Leona and her best friend, Yvette, were helping out at a yard sale to make money for their school talent show. They were selling things Leona's family didn't use anymore.

"All of my friends are talented," Leona continued. "You can act, and Maria is a math whiz, but I'm not talented at all."

"You can sing," said Yvette.

"Yes, but I sound like a frog," Leona laughed.

Yvette laughed and said, "You're funny, Leona, and that's a talent!"

Read the question and choose your answer:

How do you think Yvette feels about Leona?

a. Yvette likes Leona.
b. Yvette dislikes Leona.
c. Yvette likes Maria better than Leona.

46

Screener Passage 3

4 reading passages guide you in selecting the appropriate reading levels for your students.

20 Levels in 5 Convenient Packages

Set	Readability Level	Interest Level
Levels A–B	Kindergarten	Primary/Intermediate Newcomers in Middle School
Levels C–H	Grade 1	Primary/Intermediate
Levels I–L	Grade 2	Intermediate/Middle School
Levels M–P	Grade 3	Intermediate/Middle School
Levels Q–T	Grade 4-5	Middle School

One Level at a Glance

5 High-Interest Readers,
Each with its own Teaching Booklet!

Math

Science

Social Studies

Fiction

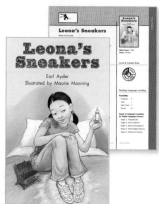

With Student-Friendly Reading Strategy Cards. Teacher notes on the back!

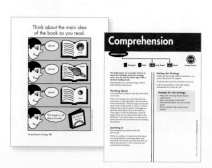

In a Convenient Storage Tub!

Engaging Student Components Motivate Readers

Nonfiction genres and text features teach students to navigate content-area reading.

Skating Tricks

Like skateboarders, inline skaters also do tricks on a ramp. Many of the tricks send the skater high into the air.

One inline skating trick is called a *360*. When skaters do a 360, they spin completely around, as if they are skating in a circle. Inline skaters need special gear to keep them safe. This gear protects them when they are doing tricks such as the 360.

helmet

knee pads

elbow pads

Interest-grabbing topics with carefully controlled readability.

Level O

Reading Characteristics
- 1700 to 1900 words for fiction
- 1400 to 1600 words for nonfiction
- Average sentence length: 14 words
- Interest level is intermediate/middle school
- Detailed descriptions emphasized
- Many opportunities for reader to use inference
- Complicated issues introduced: war, death, freedom, justice
- Chapter books introduced
- Text-picture match that enhances text
- Nonfiction books in this level introduce maps with complex compass rose, tables with 4 rows, and cross sections

Language-Building Characteristics
- Reading vocabulary focuses on early grade 3 words
- Many words have more than three syllables
- Variety of sentence adverbials in initial position (e.g., *Honestly*, we don't need any help.)
- Habitual past tense with would (e.g., Sometimes she would go to the candy store on Sundays.)
- Sentences in parentheses
- Hyphenated adjectives with number (e.g., three-bedroom house)
- Complex sentences with as if
- Multiple-meaning words with two uses within text

Word Study
- Multiple-meaning words
- Adverbs
- Prefix re-
- Nouns
- Consonant Doubling

Relate each book to your grade-level content standards with the list printed on the back cover of content-area books.

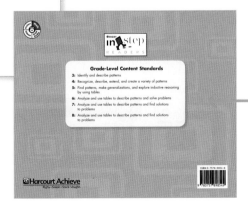

in Step READERS

Grade-Level Content Standards

3: Identify and describe patterns
4: Recognize, describe, extend, and create a variety of patterns
5: Find patterns, make generalizations, and explore inductive reasoning by using tables
6: Analyze and use tables to describe patterns and solve problems
7: Analyze and use tables to describe patterns and find solutions to problems
8: Analyze and use tables to describe patterns and find solutions to problems

Harcourt Achieve
Rigby • Saxon • Steck-Vaughn

Skills in the three key competencies are printed inside the front cover to help you plan lessons.

Think about the main idea of the book as you read.

Comprehension Strategy **10**

The student-friendly illustration makes the reading strategy accessible and easy to remember.

Comprehension

LITERACY LEVEL

 Emergent    Early   Early Fluent   Fluent

C10
Strategy Card No.

A quick, three-step process for teaching the strategy is on the back of each card, providing convenient instruction at point of use.

The following is an example of how to teach this strategy using the strategy card. You can use the same idea with a leveled reading book.

Demonstrate how to use this strategy with the following three-step process.

Thinking Aloud

First model how to find the main idea of the book as you read.

While I am reading, I try to think about how the information on each page relates to the entire book. Point to the first box. These two pages are about the planet Earth. I will keep that in mind as I continue reading. Point to the second box. These pages are about the planet Saturn. Point to the third box. These pages are about the planet Mars. All of the pages we have seen are about planets. Point to the fourth box. Since Earth, Saturn, and Mars are all planets, the main idea of this book must be something about planets.

Zooming In

Next summarize your think-aloud with fewer words.

While I am reading, it is important to think about how the information on each page relates to the entire book. Knowing the main idea of the book can help me pay attention to what is important and understand the book better.

Stating the Strategy

Finally state the strategy clearly for students as you point to the pictures for support.

Think about the main idea of the book as you read.

Look for opportunities to have each student demonstrate this strategy for you.

Prompts for This Strategy

- What is the one thing that this book is mainly about?
- What is the big idea in this book?
- What does the author want you to think about?
- Tell me what the book is about in one sentence.

Teaching Booklets with a Teacher Focus

Convenient Format

- Grab-and-go booklets are easy to tote and easy to hold.
- Booklets are bookroom-friendly!

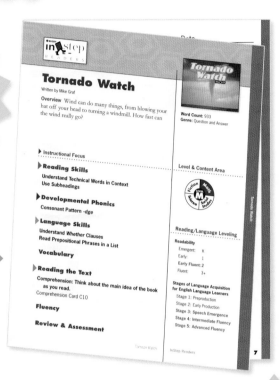

Tornado Watch
Written by Mike Graf

Overview Wind can do many things, from blowing your hat off your head to turning a windmill. How fast can the wind really go?

Word Count: 933
Genre: Question and Answer

▶ **Instructional Focus**

▶ **Reading Skills**
Understand Technical Words in Context
Use Subheadings

▶ **Developmental Phonics**
Consonant Pattern -dge

▶ **Language Skills**
Understand Whether Clauses
Read Prepositional Phrases in a List

Vocabulary

▶ **Reading the Text**
Comprehension: Think about the main idea of the book as you read.
Comprehension Card C10

Fluency

Review & Assessment

Level & Content Area

Reading/Language Leveling

Readability
Emergent: K
Early: 1
Early Fluent: 2
Fluent: 3+

Stages of Language Acquisition for English Language Learners
Stage 1: Preproduction
Stage 2: Early Production
Stage 3: Speech Emergence
Stage 4: Intermediate Fluency
Stage 5: Advanced Fluency

Clear Lesson Path in 35–45 Minutes a Day

Day One	Day Two
Before Reading: 10 – 15 minutes	After Reading: 45 minutes
During Reading: 15 – 20 minutes	

**Identifies skills in three key
competencies for the lesson.**

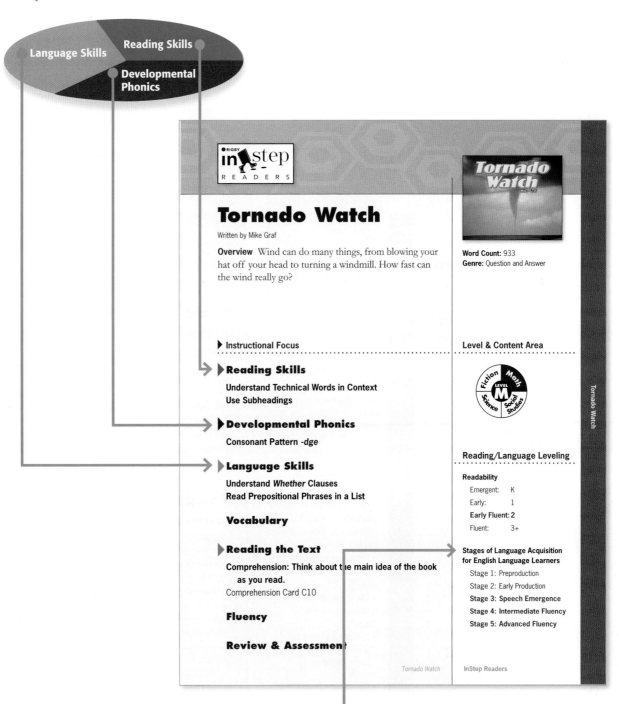

Language Skills

Reading Skills

Developmental
Phonics

RIGBY inStep READERS

Tornado Watch

Written by Mike Graf

Overview Wind can do many things, from blowing your
hat off your head to turning a windmill. How fast can
the wind really go?

Word Count: 933
Genre: Question and Answer

▶ Instructional Focus

Level & Content Area

Fiction Math
LEVEL **M**
Science Social Studies

▶ **Reading Skills**

Understand Technical Words in Context
Use Subheadings

▶ **Developmental Phonics**

Consonant Pattern -dge

Reading/Language Leveling

▶ **Language Skills**

Understand *Whether* Clauses
Read Prepositional Phrases in a List

Readability
Emergent: K
Early: 1
Early Fluent: 2
Fluent: 3+

Vocabulary

▶ **Reading the Text**

Comprehension: Think about the main idea of the book
  as you read.
Comprehension Card C10

**Stages of Language Acquisition
for English Language Learners**
Stage 1: Preproduction
Stage 2: Early Production
Stage 3: Speech Emergence
Stage 4: Intermediate Fluency
Stage 5: Advanced Fluency

Fluency

Review & Assessment

Tornado Watch   **InStep Readers**

Supports use with English Language
Learners by identifying appropriate
Stages of Language Acquisition

Before Reading

Introduce and model skills to prepare students for encountering each skill in the book.

Dual Path for Differentiated Instructio
Build background with all students while meeting their unique learning needs.

Content Standards
Supports teachers in connecting the text to the content standards of each student's grade

---

before
READING

Grade-Level Content Standards

Help students build background knowledge appropriate to their grade levels prior to reading. This book presents content relating to the following grade-level standards:

Grade 2:
• Identify likelihood of an event

Grade 3:
• Determine likelihood of an event

Grade 4:
• Compare the likelihood of events

Grade 5:
• Calculate or estimate the probability of an event

Grade 6:
• Calculate or estimate the probability of events

Grade 7:
• Calculate or estimate the probability of events and make convincing arguments

Grade 8:
• Calculate or estimate the probability of events to make predictions and decisions

Build Background

For English Language Learners	For Struggling Readers
Display photographs of tornadoes. Explain that tornadoes are windstorms with air that spins around very fast. Have students act out being tornadoes by spinning around. Ask *Have you ever been in a windstorm?* Explain that they will read a book about tornadoes.	Discuss tornadoes with students. Invite students to describe the scenes from movies or any personal experiences with windstorms they may have had. Explain that they will be reading a book that provides facts and information about tornadoes.

Reading Skills

Understand Technical Words in Context

• Engage students in a discussion about computers. Say *When I am working on the computer, I use the keyboard to type words.* Write the sentence on chart paper and underline *keyboard*. Say *The word* keyboard *is a word we use when we are talking about computers.*

• Explain that computers, sports, and other subjects have special words. Point out that often the words around the special word help us understand what it means. Invite volunteers to identify the phrase *type words,* which explain the term *keyboard.*

• Encourage volunteers to talk about favorite computer games or hobbies. Write any sentences they use that include technical words for that topic. Help students identify them.

Use Subheadings

• Show the subheading on page 22 of *Tornado Watch.* Explain that subheadings are small sections within a larger section. Say *A* subheading *helps a reader find information quickly. It lets the reader know what kind of information is in that section. When I read, I look for subheadings so that I can quickly find the information I want.*

• Encourage students to look for subheadings as they read.

2

Tornado Watch

▶ Developmental Phonics

Consonant Pattern *-dge*

- Write the word *badge* on chart paper. Underline the letters *dge* as you say the sounds. Say *The letters* d, g, e *often make the sound* /j/. *If I see a word with* -dge, *I know I need to make the sound* /j/. Ask students to chime in as you repeat the word *badge*.
- Tell students they will read words with *-dge* in the book.
- Invite students to suggest other words that end with *-dge*. Write each word on the chart paper and help volunteers use each one in a sentence.

▶ Language Skills

Understand *Whether* Clauses

- Write the sentence *Whether Lorenz plays the drums or the trumpet, he always plays well.* Read it aloud. Say *The main idea is Lorenz plays well.*
- Underline *whether* and circle *drums* and *trumpet*. Say *The word* whether *shows that we are talking about two different situations. It doesn't matter if Lorenz plays the drums or the trumpet because he always plays well.* Point out the comma.
- Help students create sentences with *whether*. Provide prompts, such as *Whether it's cloudy or sunny. . .* Help students determine the main idea.

Read Prepositional Phrases in a List

- Write the sentence *The fox ran under the fence, through the woods, and into the river.* Underline the three prepositional phrases. Say *The fox ran in three different places.* Repeat the sentence, emphasizing the prepositional phrases. Circle the commas. Say *These words are in a list, so we put commas between them.*
- Provide prompts, such as *The man walked. . .* Help students finish the sentence with three prepositional phrases in a list. Invite a student to circle them in the sentence.

Developmental Phonics/ Word Study Sequence:

Level L
- Vowel Patterns

Level M
- **Consonant Patterns**

Level N
- Adjectives
- Verbs
- Prepositions
- Contractions
- Prefix *un-*

Developmental Phonics

Developmental phonics supports teachers in matching phonics skills to students' reading levels using a research-based sequence.

InStep Readers　3

During Reading

Begin the reading process by previewing, setting a purpose for reading, and building vocabulary.

Dual Path for Differentiated Instruction

Build a solid vocabulary foundation for English language learners and expand struggling readers' understanding of vocabulary.

---

during READING

Book Talk

Comprehension and Vocabulary Support: Use these prompts to establish a comprehension framework for students' reading of the text and to elicit or supply missing vocabulary. If students are unable to answer a question, support them by providing and explaining vocabulary.

SET PURPOSE
- Read the title and have students point out the author's name.
- Have students predict what a tornado watch might be. Then display the title page and allow students to adjust their predictions. Ask students to set a purpose for reading, such as finding out new facts about tornadoes.

Vocabulary		Reading Prompts
▶ For All	**▶ For ELL**	
contents		**TITLE PAGE** *How can the contents page help us?*
tornado windstorm	clouds spinning	**PAGES 2–3** *A tornado is a windstorm. Where do you think a tornado starts? Where does a spinning tornado move?*
region Tornado Alley	Midwest Gulf of Mexico	**PAGES 4–5** *Which region is most likely to have tornadoes? When do you think they usually form?*
season likely	winter probability observe	**PAGES 6–7** *Scientists observe tornadoes. What months have a higher probability of tornadoes hitting? Do you think it's likely there are tornadoes in December?*
Fujita Scale strength	measures agreed	**PAGES 10–12** *One tool that measures a tornado is called a "turtle" by scientists. Most people have agreed to use the Fujita Scale to measure the strength of a tornado.*
Tri-State Super Outbreak	occurred	**PAGES 14–15** *The Tri-State tornado killed more people than any other tornado in history. The Super Outbreak occurred on April 3 and 4 in 1974.*
compass weather vane	compass thermometer	**PAGES 18–19** *What do you think a storm chaser does? Storm chasers use a weather radio, cameras, a compass, a weather vane, a thermometer, and maps to help them.*
watch warning	weather reports	**PAGES 22–23** *Why do you think the National Weather Service gives weather reports on the TV and radio? Weather reporters use the words tornado watch and tornado warning.*

4

Tornado Watch

Vocabulary

For English Language Learners	For Struggling Readers
Ask students to act out terms from the book, such as **tornado** or lightning. Ask if they have ever been in a bad storm. Encourage them to tell what safety tips they followed. Ask them how this might help keep them safe during a tornado.	Discuss different kinds of weather and **storms** with students. What storms have they experienced? Encourage students to compare characteristics of other **weather** and storms with tornadoes.

▶ Reading the Text ◀

Concepts of Print Card C10

Before students begin reading the book, introduce the Reading Strategy Card by following the instructions on the back. Display the card and encourage students to refer to it as they read.

Reading with the Reading Strategy Card

• Provide copies of the book to students. Have each student read silently at his or her own pace while in the group. Tap a student on the shoulder to hear him or her read a page as you observe.

• Remind students to use the reading strategy as they read.

• Later have students reread the book to practice the strategy.

Reading Strategy Coaching Tip:

To check that students are thinking about the main idea of the book, ask them how they would summarize the book for a friend or classmate, in their own words.

Fluency ◀

Model reading with appropriate phrasing. Write this sentence from page 3 with slash marks on chart paper: *A tornado is a windstorm/that starts inside a cloud/and moves over land/in a spinning motion.* Read the sentence, pausing at each slash mark. Say *When I read, I pause between groups of words so they make sense together.* Have students repeat. Write down a sentence students suggest. Have students add slash marks between phrases.

InStep Readers 5

Scaffold Reading
Use the visual support of the Reading Strategy Cards to build students' command of reading strategies.

Build Reading Power
Focus on five core fluency skills to practice reading aloud and build reading power.

Assess What You Teach!

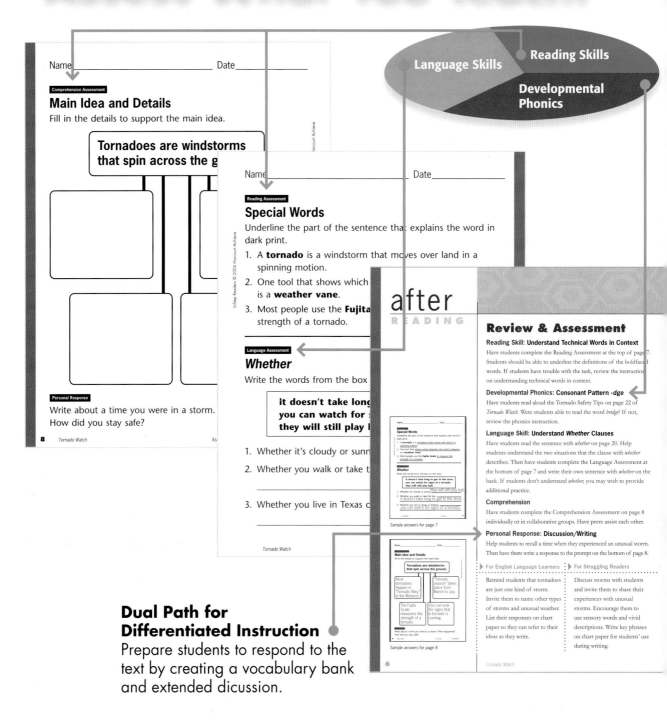

Language Skills

Reading Skills

Developmental Phonics

Name _____ Date _____

Comprehension Assessment

Main Idea and Details

Fill in the details to support the main idea.

Tornadoes are windstorms that spin across the g[round]

Personal Response

Write about a time you were in a storm. How did you stay safe?

8   *Tornado Watch*

Name _____ Date _____

Reading Assessment

Special Words

Underline the part of the sentence that explains the word in dark print.

1. A **tornado** is a windstorm that moves over land in a spinning motion.
2. One tool that shows which [direction the wind is blowing] is a **weather vane**.
3. Most people use the **Fujita** [Scale to measure the] strength of a tornado.

Language Assessment

Whether

Write the words from the box on the lines.

> **it doesn't take long** [to get to the store,]
> **you can watch for** [signs of a tornado,]
> **they will still play** [ball]

1. Whether it's cloudy or sunn[y,]
2. Whether you walk or take t[he bus,]

_____

3. Whether you live in Texas o[r]

_____

Tornado Watch

after
READING

Review & Assessment

Reading Skill: Understand Technical Words in Context

Have students complete the Reading Assessment at the top of page 7. Students should be able to underline the definitions of the boldfaced words. If students have trouble with the task, review the instruction on understanding technical words in context.

Developmental Phonics: Consonant Pattern -dge

Have students read aloud the Tornado Safety Tips on page 22 of *Tornado Watch*. Were students able to read the word *bridge*? If not, review the phonics instruction.

Language Skill: Understand *Whether* Clauses

Have students read the sentence with *whether* on page 20. Help students understand the two situations that the clause with *whether* describes. Then have students complete the Language Assessment at the bottom of page 7 and write their own sentence with *whether* on the back. If students don't understand *whether*, you may wish to provide additional practice.

Comprehension

Have students complete the Comprehension Assessment on page 8 individually or in collaborative groups. Have peers assist each other.

Personal Response: Discussion/Writing

Help students to recall a time when they experienced an unusual storm. Then have them write a response to the prompt on the bottom of page 8.

▶ For English Language Learners	▶ For Struggling Readers
Remind students that tornadoes are just one kind of storm. Invite them to name other types of storms and unusual weather. List their responses on chart paper so they can refer to their ideas as they write.	Discuss storms with students and invite them to share their experiences with unusual storms. Encourage them to use sensory words and vivid descriptions. Write key phrases on chart paper for students' use during writing.

Tornado Watch   6

Dual Path for Differentiated Instruction

Prepare students to respond to the text by creating a vocabulary bank and extended dicussion.

Genres and Nonfiction Features

Genres and nonfiction features are introduced at specific levels of *InStep Readers*. The chart below is a quick reference for what students will encounter at each level.

Level A

Genres

Fiction: Realistic Fiction

Nonfiction: Expository

Nonfiction: Personal Narrative

Nonfiction Features

Nonfiction features begin at Level D.

Level B

Fiction: Animal Fantasy

Level C

Nonfiction: Personal Narrative

Level D

Informational Fiction

 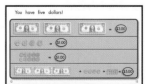

materials list

Genres

Fiction: Play

Fiction: Mystery

Nonfiction: Procedural

Nonfiction: Question and Answer

Nonfiction: Picture Dictionary

Nonfiction Features

contents page   recipe

picture glossary

 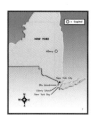

map with simple key
and compass rose

Level E

Level F

Genres

Nonfiction Features

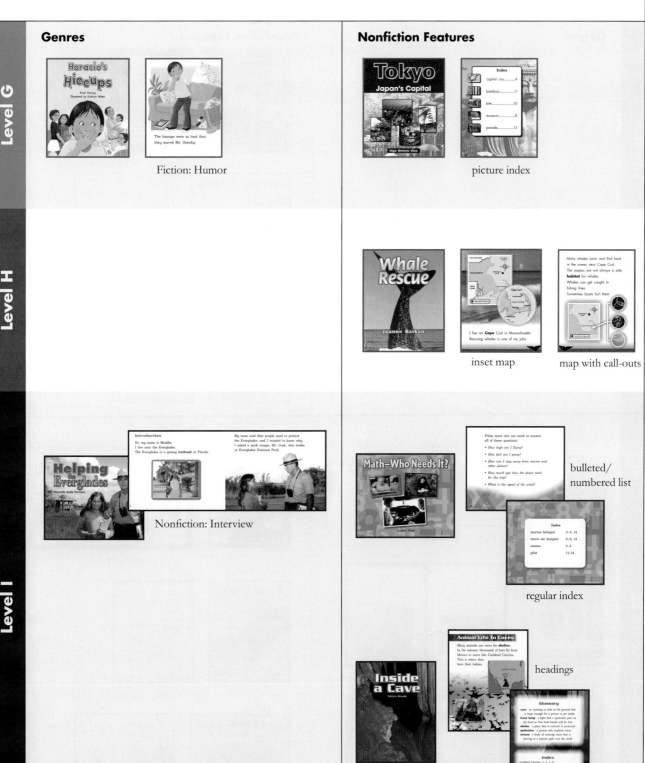

Level G

Fiction: Humor

picture index

Level H

inset map

map with call-outs

Level I

Nonfiction: Interview

bulleted/ numbered list

regular index

headings

regular glossary

Genres

Nonfiction Features

diagram with callouts

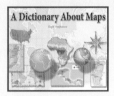
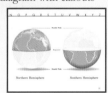

caption

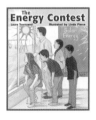

flow chart with labels

Level J

Level K

Level L

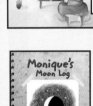

Fiction: Folktale

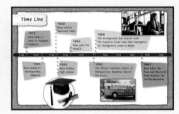

horizontal time line

Nonfiction: Journal/Observation Log

sentence-length captions

Nonfiction: Biography

bird's-eye view

Genres

Fiction: Fantasy

Nonfiction: Encyclopedia

Nonfiction Features

e-mail/letter within text

simple sidebar

subheading

size-comparison diagram

diagram with labels

sidebar with bulleted list

satellite image

table with 2 rows

simple floor plan

Genres

Level O

Chapter Books

Level P

Fiction: Adventure

Nonfiction Features

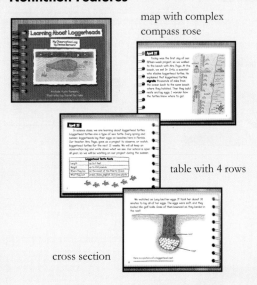

map with complex
compass rose

table with 4 rows

cross section

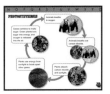

simple flow chart with
sentence-length captions

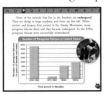

bar graph

circle graph

captions of
several sentences
that extend text

Genres

Level Q

Fiction: Science Fiction

Fiction: Blended Genres

Level R

Fiction: Diary

Nonfiction Features

caption with questions requiring picture interpretation

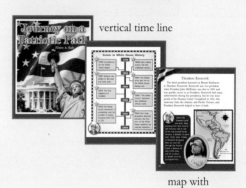

vertical time line

map with multiple-element key

scale diagram

map with scale

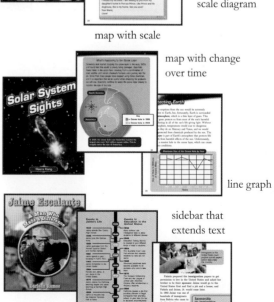

map with change over time

line graph

sidebar that extends text

parallel time line

Genres

Fiction: Historical Fiction

Nonfiction Features

 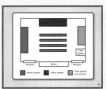

complex floor plan
(floor plan with key)

comparative visual
representation of
information

microscopic image

Nonfiction: Persuasive

double bar graph

table with
2-row head

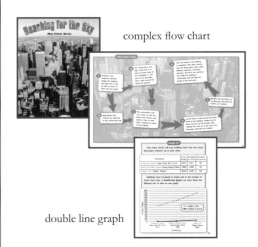

complex flow chart

double line graph

Level S

Level T

▶ PROFESSIONAL HANDBOOK

Differentiating Instruction for Literacy Levels

Literacy development is a process that unfolds in four discernable phases:

- Emergent
- Early
- Early Fluent
- Fluent

A student's literacy level is not determined by age or even by grade level. Literacy level is about a student's individual place in reading development. *InStep Readers* ensures that students are reading at the right level at the right time.

Emergent

Emergent level readers understand that print carries meaningful messages and begin to learn the basic concepts about books, print, letters, and sounds. These readers benefit from sentence patterns and direct text-picture match in Levels A and B.

Early

Early level readers have print awareness and know that books have exact and unchanging messages. They know that reading is a meaning-making process that uses problem-solving skills. Readers at this level thrive with short books that are highly supportive and have direct-to-supportive text-picture match in Levels C–I.

Early Fluent

Early fluent readers have an array of problem-solving skills to use as they read and begin to use multiple clues to make meaning. They rely less on illustrations as a clue to text meaning. Readers at this literacy level can grasp books' main ideas and their emotional impact and enjoy challenging content at Levels J–M.

Fluent

Fluent readers can make sense of complex books that are longer. These readers adapt strategies flexibly and can orchestrate all the clues available to make meaning. Fluent readers self-correct flexibly and efficiently and are prepared for the more sophisticated content presented in Levels N–T.

Differentiating Instruction for Struggling Readers

Leveled Reading for Struggling Readers

When struggling readers understand and are engaged in the books they read, they become successful readers. Students experience frustration when asked to read books beyond their abilities and will become reluctant to try again. These students often have had little to no exposure to reading early on in the home and haven't built vocabulary or developed reading strategies.

Good comprehension requires discussions that support the understanding of specific texts. Teachers can then support a struggling reader's strategy development by gradually providing texts at increasingly challenging levels of difficulty.

InStep Readers are the leveled texts that struggling readers need to succeed. Teachers can work with students in small homogeneous groups with the same book at lower levels or in small mixed groups with different books at higher levels.

Motivating Struggling Readers

A reader who struggles to understand what he or she is reading or who has difficulty making personal connections to the text is often frustrated or uninterested in reading and loses motivation. Without motivation, students read less and fail to improve.

InStep Readers provide a wide range of age-appropriate fiction plots and high-interest content-area topics. Background-building supports making personal connections to the text, providing motivation.

Direct Reading Skills Instruction

Struggling readers' difficulties often start at the word level. Readers at the emergent and early levels of literacy need exposure to and instruction in high-frequency words in order to build a core bank of words that they can recognize in any context.

Explicit, Systematic Instruction for Struggling Readers

Struggling readers are best supported with direct, explicit, systematic instruction of skills and strategies. Then, if what they learn and how they learn is purposeful, they will succeed.

Cross-Checking

Cross-checking is the flexible, simultaneous, and fluent use of all three cueing systems: structural (grammar), semantic (meaning), and decoding (sounds/letters). Successful readers have developed strategies for figuring out words they encounter and can't immediately recognize, and are able to self-monitor and know when to switch back and forth among these three in order to make meaning from text.

Struggling readers often choose one cueing system, and regardless of whether it helps them successfully navigate text, will continue to use that single system. These students must be taught how to use these three cueing systems flexibly through reading, language, and phonics instruction.

Struggling readers have difficulty understanding the organization of genres and text structures. And while all readers can benefit from instruction in nonfiction features, it is critical for struggling readers who have few resources for figuring out these challenges on their own.

InStep Readers levels A through I focus on high-frequency words, exposing struggling readers to these words repeatedly. This program also provides explicit instruction in text types and genres, as well as nonfiction text features. New genres and features are gradually introduced across levels, allowing students to learn how to master each one in context before moving to the next level.

Direct Developmental Phonics Instruction

Readers at the emergent and early levels of literacy have difficulty decoding words. A student needs to learn phonics skills that pertain to texts at his or her reading level to decode text fluently and build comprehension. At higher literacy levels, struggling readers have difficulty deconstructing words (using prefixes and suffixes to make meaning) and understanding parts of speech and other components that are the building blocks of our language.

InStep Readers provide explicit instruction in phonemic awareness, phonics, and word study at a rate that is developmentally appropriate.

Direct Language Skills Instruction

Unfamiliar grammatical structures can prove difficult for struggling readers. One way to foster growth is to control the sentence structures they read at each level, gradually increasing complexity.

Each reading level of *InStep Readers* is carefully controlled for sentence length, sentence complexity, and grammatical structure. New grammatical structures are taught before reading.

Direct Vocabulary Instruction

Students with little exposure to reading have not built the vocabulary that prepares them to read. The common literary language of fiction is unfamiliar to struggling readers, as is the basic vocabulary needed for academic success in the content areas.

InStep Readers introduces key vocabulary during a preview of the book. Then, depending on students' needs, you can discuss vocabulary before or after reading. Before reading, help students build knowledge of words and concepts from the book. After reading, enable students to revisit key vocabulary in context and to extend to related words.

Developing Reading Strategies with Struggling Readers

Successful readers acquire reading strategies through frequent reading. Struggling readers need instruction in these strategies. The Reading Strategy Cards provided with InStep Readers offer explicit strategy instruction and are introduced before reading and reinforced during reading.

Building Comprehension with Graphic Organizers

Struggling readers need tools to improve their understanding and retention of what they have read. Graphic organizers help struggling readers compare text content and structure and focus their thoughts. The Teaching Booklet for each Reader provides a comprehension assessment graphic organizer specific to the Reader's text type.

Building Fluency for Struggling Readers

Slow, stilted reading hinders comprehension. Being able to read fluently can enable struggling readers to read for meaning and to check what they read against their language knowledge.

InStep Readers supports fluency through guided repeated readings of texts and direct instruction and practice with fluency skills.

Five Core Fluency Skills

- Use punctuation when reading aloud
- Stress words in bold and italics when reading aloud
- Change your voice for different characters
- Read aloud with appropriate phrasing
- Change your voice to show characters' feelings

Differentiating Instruction for English Language Learners

Leveled Reading for English Language Learners

ELLs proceed along distinct phases within the language development and literacy development processes. The key is to match the level of reading ability to the text level of language ability. *InStep Readers* guide you in understanding the Stages of Language Acquisition appropriate for each text level. Work with small groups who have similar needs and are able to read at the same instructional level.

Stages of Language Acquisition

STAGE 1: Preproduction Students comprehend a limited amount of everyday English and communicate primarily through gestures and may produce one-word responses in English if at all.

STAGE 2: Early Production Some social conversation is understood, but students' comprehension of academic conversation is limited. Basic ideas and needs are conveyed with basic expressions, though reliance on gestures to communicate is still strong. Simple phrases are used as well as some academic words used in isolation.

STAGE 3: Speech Emergence Students understand social and academic conversation with the occasional lapse. Speech contains errors that may hinder communication; however, students participate in everyday conversation and produce longer, complete phrases and some sentences. Students rely on high-frequency words and uses academic language. Some ideas are communicated unsuccessfully due to a lack of vocabulary.

STAGE 4: Intermediate Fluency Students rarely experience a lack of understanding in social and academic conversations. Speech contains minor errors that don't affect communication, and some idioms and complex sentences are used. Everyday and academic vocabulary allows for successful communication, though students must occasionally work around unknown words.

STAGE 5: Advanced Fluency Students understand social and academic conversations without difficulty. Ideas are conveyed successfully in English, and speech appears to be fluent and effortless. Vocabulary, academic language, and idioms are used as well as native-speaking peers.

Building Background for ELLs

Unfamiliar concepts present problems for ELLs. A lack of context in which to place text leaves little room for comprehension. Build background on these unfamiliar concepts to help ELLs learn new vocabulary before they read each title offered in *InStep Readers*.

Direct Reading Skills Instruction

ELLs need exposure to and direct instruction in high-frequency words in order to build a bank of words that they can recognize in any context. In addition, ELLs have difficulty understanding the organization of text genres and structures. Nonfiction features such as lists and charts can also pose a great challenge. *InStep Readers* Levels A through I have a focus on high-frequency words. The program also provides explicit instruction in text types, genres, and nonfiction text features, introducing these new elements gradually across levels.

Direct Developmental Phonics Instruction

ELLs possess some knowledge about how sounds and letters (or symbols) correspond to make words in their primary languages. ELLs—especially those with exposure to literacy instruction in their primary language—can use their knowledge of their home language and transfer as much of it as possible to English. Use *InStep Readers* to provide direct, explicit instruction in phonemic awareness, developmental phonics, and word study before reading.

Phonics Instruction for ELLs

ELLs need developmental phonics instruction appropriate to their literacy levels and Stages of Language Acquisition. Phonics instruction does not relate to age or to grade level—it relates to the reading level of each student.

Building Fluency for English Language Learners

Being able to read quickly with few mistakes can help ELLs improve comprehension and feel more confident. Practice with fluency skills should be short but frequent.

Five Core Fluency Skills

- Use punctuation when reading aloud
- Stress words in bold and italics when reading aloud
- Change your voice for different characters
- Read aloud with appropriate phrasing
- Change your voice to show characters' feelings

Building Comprehension with Graphic Organizers

ELLs need visual support to improve their comprehension and to help them organize their thoughts.

The Teaching Booklet for each Reader provides a comprehension assessment graphic organizer. These organizers make it easier for students to make sense of the information they have read and to focus their thoughts.

Direct Language Skills Instruction

Unfamiliar literary and grammatical structures and academic English can hinder comprehension for ELLs. By controlling sentence structure and gradually increasing sentence complexity, you can help ELLs acquire the language skills they need to improve comprehension. Each reading level of *InStep Readers* is carefully controlled for sentence length, sentence complexity, and grammatical structure. New structures are taught using gestures, pictures, and actions to provide comprehensible input critical to meeting the needs of ELLs.

Direct Vocabulary Instruction

ELLs need to build their social and academic vocabularies to become fluent readers and speakers. To address this need to develop vocabulary, *InStep Readers* introduces key vocabulary during a preview of the book. Before reading, help students build basic knowledge of words and concepts from the book. After reading, revisit key vocabulary and concepts in context and extend to related words. For students in Stages 1–2, use visual support to provide comprehensible input.

Developing Reading Strategies with ELLs

ELLs need explicit instruction in using reading strategies. The Reading Strategy Cards provided with *InStep Readers* offer explicit instruction to facilitate comprehension. Teachers can explain the strategy first, and students practice the strategy as they read.

▶ASSESSMENT

Screener for Initial Reading Level Placement

This Screener allows you to quickly approximate the instructional reading level for each student using the following three Pre-screener questions, four reading passages, and comprehension questions.

Administering the Screener

Ask the student each of the Pre-screener questions below. If the student does not respond correctly to any of the questions, stop and place the student at Level A. If the student responds correctly to one or more questions, administer Screener Passage 1.

1. Write the letters *m, a, s,* and *u* on a sheet of paper and show them to student. Can the student name each letter? __Yes __No

2. Refer to the sheet of paper from question 1 and ask the student to make the sound of each letter. Can the student make each sound? __Yes __No

3. Place a book in front of the student. Ask the student to pick it up and get ready to read. Does the student hold the book correctly and turn to the first page? __Yes __No

Step 1 **Reading Accuracy Check**

Have the student read Passage 1 aloud to you. Make a tally mark every time the student misses a word or substitutes an incorrect word without self-correcting. Speakers of non-standard dialects may have the same issues as English language learners, which you may want to consider as you tally errors. If any error sounds like the student's oral English, do not make a tally mark.

Step 2 **Determining Reading Level**

Count the number of errors tallied. Use the chart on the Screener Administration Record to determine the student's Level.

Step 3 **Comprehension Check**

Ask the student to read and respond to the comprehension question at the end of the reading passage. If the student answers correctly, start him or her at the Level determined in Step 2. If the student answers incorrectly, place the student at the Level immediately before it.

Answers to comprehension questions:

1. B   2. B   3. A   4. B

Screener Administration Record

Pre-screener

Check all parts administered

If student answers 1 or more Pre-Screener questions correctly...	administer Screener Passage 1.

Screener

☐	If student reads **Passage 1** and makes more than 3 errors . . . 3 errors . . . 2 errors . . . 1 or no errors . . . Did student respond to question correctly?	start student at Level A. start student at Level B. start student at Level C. administer Screener Passage 2. __Yes __No
☐	If student reads **Passage 2** and makes more than 8 errors . . . 6–8 errors . . . 4–5 errors . . . 3 errors . . . 2 or fewer errors . . . Did student respond to question correctly?	start student at Level D. start student at Level G. start student at Level H. start student at Level I. administer Screener Passage 3. __Yes __No
☐	If student reads **Passage 3** and makes more than 20 errors . . . 15–20 errors . . . 10–14 errors . . . 5–9 errors . . . 4 or fewer errors . . . Did student respond to question correctly?	start student at Level J. start student at Level M. start student at Level N. start student at Level O. administer Screener Passage 4. __Yes __No
☐	If student reads **Passage 4** and makes more than 16 errors . . . 12–15 errors . . . 6–11 errors . . . 1–5 errors . . . 0 errors . . . Did student respond to question correctly?	start student at Level P. start student at Level Q. start student at Level R. start student at Level S. start student at Level T. __Yes __No

Teacher Notes:

Carlos and Dad

Carlos and Dad are in a car.

Dad is driving.
Carlos is looking
at the trees.

Choose the correct answer.

What is Carlos doing?

a. Carlos is driving.

b. Carlos is looking at the trees.

c. Carlos is reading.

Mariela's Trip

Mariela was very happy that she was going on a trip.

It was her first trip to New Mexico.

She was with her mother, father, and cousin Paloma, who sat next to her.

Choose the correct answer:

Why do you think Mariela was happy?

a. She was with her brother.

b. This was her first trip to a new place.

c. She likes her cousin Paloma.

Leona's Talent

"I wish I had talent," Leona sighed. Leona and her best friend, Yvette, were helping out at a yard sale to make money for their school talent show. They were selling things Leona's family didn't use anymore.

"All of my friends are talented," Leona continued. "You can act, and Maria is a math whiz, but I'm not talented at all."

"You can sing," said Yvette.

"Yes, but I sound like a frog," Leona laughed.

Yvette laughed and said, "You're funny, Leona, and that's a talent!"

Read the question and choose your answer:

How do you think Yvette feels about Leona?

a. Yvette likes Leona.

b. Yvette dislikes Leona.

c. Yvette likes Maria better than Leona.

The Mount Rushmore Memorial

Here we are in South Dakota, home of the Mount Rushmore Memorial, and I think you should definitely take a picture of this amazing sight! This memorial is a group of large stone carvings on a granite cliff. The carvings are the faces of four presidents: George Washington, Thomas Jefferson, Theodore Roosevelt, and Abraham Lincoln.

The work was created by an American sculptor. He and his assistants used drills and dynamite to blast through the rock and shape the faces. The project began in 1927 and took nearly 14 years to complete. Unfortunately, the sculptor died in 1941 before the work was finished. His son completed the job.

Choose the correct answer to the following question:

Why do you think this sculpture is called a "memorial"?

a. It took 14 years to complete.

b. It was built to remember American presidents.

c. It is so big that no one can forget it.

Oral Language Rubric

Beginning	**STAGE 1:** Pre-production	**Comprehension** Understands little of everyday English.
		Message Communicates primarily through gestures or single-word utterances. Able to communicate only the most rudimentary needs.
		Fluency and Sentence Structure Produces little, if any, spoken English.
Beginning	**STAGE 2:** Early Production	**Comprehension** Understands some social conversation but limited academic conversation.
		Message Uses routine expressions to convey basic needs and ideas. To some extent, continues to rely on gestures to communicate.
		Fluency and Sentence Structure Uses some basic words and simple phrases.
		Word Choice and Academic Language Relies on routine language expressions. May use some academic words in isolation.
Intermediate	**STAGE 3:** Speech Emergence	**Comprehension** Understands most of what is said in social and academic conversation but exhibits occasional lack of understanding.
		Message Participates in everyday conversations about familiar topics. Although speech contains errors that sometimes hinder communication, child can often convey his or her basic message.
		Fluency and Sentence Structure Produces longer, complete phrases and some sentences.
		Word Choice and Academic Language Relies on high-frequency words and sometimes cannot fully communicate ideas due to a lack of sufficient vocabulary. Uses some academic language although not always successfully.
Advanced	**STAGE 4:** Intermediate Fluency	**Comprehension** Rarely experiences a lack of understanding in social and academic situations.
		Message Engages in ordinary conversation. Although errors may be present, they generally do not hinder communication. Successfully communicates most ideas to others.
		Fluency and Sentence Structure Engages in ordinary conversation with some complex sentences. Errors no longer hinder communication.
		Word Choice and Academic Language Range of vocabulary and academic language allows child to communicate well on everyday topics. Begins to use idioms. Occasionally uses inappropriate terms and/or must rephrase to work around unknown vocabulary.
Advanced	**STAGE 5:** Advanced Fluency	**Comprehension** Understands social and academic conversation without difficulty.
		Message Uses English successfully to convey his or her ideas to others.
		Fluency and Sentence Structure Speech appears to be fluent and effortless, approximating that of native-speaking peers.
		Word Choice and Academic Language Use of vocabulary, academic language, and idioms approximates that of native-speaking peers.

Reading Fluency

What Is a Fluent Reader?

Fluent readers read texts accurately and expressively by dividing the text into meaningful phrases and clauses, knowing when to pause within and at the end of sentences, and changing emphasis and tone. They make connections among the words and ideas in the text and between the text and their prior knowledge.

What Is Fluent Reading for ELLs?

Placing emphasis on reading fluency before ELLs have achieved adequate oral language fluency is counterproductive since students' oral reading relies heavily on their speaking ability. Begin assessing reading fluency with students in Stages 4 and 5 in oral language acquisition. For students in Stages 1–3, it would be impossible to distinguish between oral and reading fluency issues.

How Can Reading Fluency Be Assessed?

Reading rate can be measured by a formal assessment of timed reading. Prosodic features, the reader's ability to use expression and phrasing, can be evaluated with an informal assessment that notes observations about the student's reading.

To use the Reading Fluency Assessment (page 50), choose a Student Reader at a student's Rigby ELL Level. The student should have read the book in a group session and independently. Choose text from the middle of the book for the timed reading. Students at Rigby ELL Level F or above can be assessed for fluency.

Calculating Words Correct Per Minute

The first chart in the margin contains benchmark reading rates for on-grade-level readers. Because ELLs are usually not reading on grade level, these rates are adjusted for use with students' current reading levels. Words Correct Per Minute for ELLs (Stages 4–5) should be gauged by their current Rigby ELL Level. Target a rate for each student according to the closest Rigby ELL Level listed in the chart.

A study by the National Assessment of Educational Progress (NAEP) has found that fluent readers score higher on measures of comprehension.

Benchmarks for On-Grade-Level Readers

End of Grade	Words Correct/Minute
1	60
2	90-100
2	114
4	140
5	160

Benchmarks for English Language Learners by Rigby ELL Levels

Rigby ELL Level	Words Correct/Minute
I	60
M	90-100
P	114
T	140

Name: _____ **Grade:** _____ **Reading Level:** _____ **Date:** _____

Reading Fluency Assessment

Calculate a student's WCPM rate by timing a reading for one minute. Use a 1, 2, 3 or 4 for each descriptor. Add the ratings and divide by 6 to find the average. Check off any additional observations.

Total Words Read Per Minute (TWR) – Errors (E) = Words Correct Per Minute (WCPM)

_____ – _____ = _____
TWR – E = WCPM

Fluency Area	1	2	3	4	Additional Observatons
Expression Rating Descriptors	Monotone, word-by-word reading with no expression	Mostly word-by-word reading with little expression	Mixed word-by-word and phrased reading with some expression	Expressive reading with a consistent conversational tone	☐ Matches character's feelings ☐ Changes voice to differentiate speakers ☐ Uses volume to express emotion
				Expression Rating	
Accuracy Rating Descriptors	Frequent errors, repetitions, false starts, miscues, mispronunciations	Some errors, repetitions, false starts, miscues, mispronunciations	Occasional errors with word recognition or pronunciation	Accurate word recognition and pronunciation	☐ Reads every word; no skipping/substituting ☐ Pronounces difficult words accurately
				Accuracy Rating	
Attention to Punctuation Rating Descriptors	No attention to punctuation signals for intonation or stress	Some attention to punctuation signals for intonation or stress	Moderate attention to punctuation signals for intonation or stress	Correct intonation and stress based on pronunciation	☐ Varies volume according to print or punctuation cues ☐ Emphasizes italicized words
				Attention to Punctuation Rating	
Appropriate Phrasing Rating Descriptors	Little or no sense of phrase boundaries	Choppy reading that may not correspond to phrases	Moderate sense of proper phrasing with some misplaced pauses for breath	Generally well-phrased with correct pauses for breath	☐ Varies volume when reading phrases ☐ Takes breath at appropriate times
				Appropriate Phrasing Rating	
Smooth Reading Rating Descriptors	Laborious reading pace	Moderately slow reading pace	Mixed fast and slow reading pace	Consistent reading pace	☐ Reading sounds confident and effortless
				Smooth Reading Rating	
Comprehension Rating Descriptors	Cannot retell main idea (or plot event) or details	Retells main idea (or plot event) or some details	Retells main idea (or plot event) with one or two details	Retells main idea (or plot event) with all supporting details	☐ Recounts events in order ☐ Creates an interpretation of text
				Comprehension Rating	
		Overall Fluency Rating (Average by adding all ratings ÷ 6)			**Final Score:**

Name: _____ Grade: _____

Emergent Reading Checklist

Record the date under the appropriate observation.

Reading Skills	Observed Achievement of Skill	Observed Difficulty with Skill	Comments
Understands that writers use letter symbols to construct meaning			
Realizes that print carries a message			
Uses picture cues to comprehend text			
Demonstrates directionality (left/right)			
Demonstrates directionality (top/bottom)			
Matches spoken word to print			
Identifies some sounds			
Identifies uppercase and lowercase letter names			
Understands words are separated by spaces			
Understands that words are made up of letters that correspond to sounds			
Recognizes own name			
Recognizes and reads common environmental print			
Retells stories and rhymes			
Reads simple one-syllable and high-frequency words			
Recognizes parts of a book (cover, title, title page)			
Locates name of author and illustrator			

Name: _____ **Grade:** _____

Student Uses Strategy:
C = consistently S = sometimes R = rarely

Emergent Reading Strategy Checklist

	Reading Strategy Number and Card	Teacher Observations	Levels	Student Uses Strategy...
CP1	Look at the pictures.	Student finds meaning with picture-text match.	A–B	
CP2	Look at the words from left to right.	Student follows print from left to right. (Directionality of print)	A–B	
CP3	Point to each word as you read.	Student has one-to-one matching of voice to print and phonics clues.	A–B	
CP4	When you get to the end of a line, go to the start of the next line.	Student uses return sweep.	A–B	
CP5	Look for words you know.	Student recognizes high-frequency words.	A–H	
CP6	Check for a pattern.	Student recognizes that there is a pattern to the text that will help while reading.	C–H	
CP7	Does it sound right?	Student uses syntactic cues. (ELLs need extra support with this strategy.)	C–H	
C1	Use the pictures to help you understand the words.	Student reads a text using words and pictures.	A–B	
C2	Think about what comes next and if it makes sense.	Student predicts what words or phrases will come next.	C–H	

Name: _____ Grade: _____

Early Reading Checklist

Record the date under the appropriate observation.

Reading Skills	Observed Achievement of Skill	Observed Difficulty with Skill	Comments
Recalls facts from nonfiction text			
Participates in shared reading			
Cross-checks phonics and picture clues to problem-solve words			
Uses prior knowledge to help construct meaning			
Uses decoding skills			
Shares feelings about text			
Relies more on word cues than on picture cues			
Self-monitors by asking questions			
Responds creatively to content			
Makes some text-to-self connections			
Notices miscues and works at correcting them			
Uses context to confirm predictions			
Rereads to check meaning			
Retells longer stories in sequence with some detail			
Reads independently for pleasure			
Recognizes, reads, and writes an extended core of high-frequency words			
Uses contents page and index to locate information			

Early Reading Strategy Checklist

	Reading Strategy Number and Card	Teacher Observations	Levels	Student Uses Strategy...
CP5	Look for words you know.	Student recognizes high-frequency words.	A–H	
CP6	Check for a pattern	Student recognizes that there is a pattern to the text that will help while reading.	C–H	
CP7	Does it sound right?	Student uses syntactic cues. (ELLs need extra support with this strategy.)	C–H	
CP8	Think about the features.	Student looks at the features in a nonfiction text to help figure out what is important.	I–L	
CP9	Think about what you want to know to help you decide what part to read.	Student decides what part of the nonfiction text will provide the information needed.	I–L	
C2	Think about what comes next and if it makes sense.	Student predicts what words or phrases will come next.	C–H	
C3	Go back to the beginning of the page and try again.	Student reads for deeper meaning in context.	I–L	
C4	Think about the elements of the story.	Student thinks about story elements.	I–L	
C5	Ask yourself if what you are reading makes sense.	Student adjusts pace and monitors comprehension.	I–L	
C6	Predict what might happen next.	Student predicts what will happen.	I–L	
C7	Think about something you may have read or heard or done before.	Student uses previous experiences to help with understanding.	I–L	
C8	Think about why a character is saying or doing something.	Student interprets traits and motivations.	I–P	
C9	Make sure you have questions in your mind before, during, and after reading.	Student asks him/herself questions while reading.	I–P	

Name: _____   Grade: _____

Early Fluency Reading Checklist

Record the date under the appropriate observation.

Reading Skills	Observed Achievement of Skill	Observed Difficulty with Skill	Comments
Chooses a variety of genres for independent reading			
Uses multiple clues (semantic, syntactic, phonics) to make meaning			
Reads in phrases or chunks			
Demonstrates some problem-solving strategies when challenged by difficult text (i.e., rereads text, thinks about main idea)			
Retells stories in sequence, using details and with a strong sense of plot			
Recounts facts from informational text in a coherent manner			
Begins to have an understanding of spelling conventions			
Knows how to use an index			
Uses multiple strategies for unlocking unknown words			
Sometimes self-monitors during reading (i.e., asks questions to self)			
Monitors own writing			
Identifies some misspelled words in own writing			
Begins to write for different purposes			
Knows how to use a glossary			

Early Fluency Reading Strategy Checklist

	Reading Strategy Number and Card	Teacher Observations	Level	Student Uses Strategy...
CP8	Think about the features.	Student looks at the features in a nonfiction text to see what is important.	I–L	
CP9	Think about what you want to know to help you decide what part to read.	Student reads part of text with the information needed.	I–L	
CP 10	Preview the text before you read.	Student self-initiates text previewing.	M–P	
C3	Go back to the beginning of the page and try again.	Student reads for deeper meaning in context.	I–L	
C4	Think about the elements of the story.	Student thinks about story elements.	I–L	
C5	Ask yourself if what you are reading makes sense.	Student adjusts pace and monitors comprehension.	I–L	
C6	Predict what might happen next.	Student predicts what will happen.	I–L	
C7	Think about something you may have read or heard or done before.	Student uses previous experiences to help with understanding.	I–L	
C8	Think about why a character is saying or doing something.	Student interprets traits and motivations.	I–P	
C9	Make sure you have questions in your mind before, during, and after reading.	Student asks him/herself questions while reading.	I–P	
C10	Think about the main idea of the book as you read.	Student identifies the main idea.	M–P	
C11	Think about the important details.	Student supports and separates details.	M–P	
C12	As you read, predict events and solutions to problems.	Student creates and revises predictions.	M–P	
C13	You don't need to understand every word to understand the text.	Student reads for overall meaning, avoiding word-for-word translation.	M–P	
C14	As you read, make judgments about what you read.	Student thinks critically.	M–P	
C15	Make connections to your life, your other reading, and what you know.	Student connects text to self, text to text, and text to world.	M–P	
C16	Change your mind as you find new information in your reading.	Student revises thoughts and conclusions based on new information.	M–P	
C17	Think about what you need to remember as you continue to read.	Student sustains attention and memory over periods of time.	M–P	
C18	Make conclusions as you read.	Student draws conclusions.	M–T	

Name: _____ **Grade:** _____

Fluency Reading Checklist

Record the date under the appropriate observation.

Reading Skills	Observed Achievement of Skill	Observed Difficulty with Skill	Comments
Reads independently from variety of genres			
Self-monitors and self-corrects flexibly and efficiently			
Asks questions to confirm understanding			
Forms and supports opinions			
Uses text-to-self, text-to-text, and text-to-world connections			
Evidences a knowledge of most spelling conventions			
Listens to chapter books			
Reads chapter books independently			
Successfully problem-solves unknown words			
Adapts strategies to fulfill a range of reading purposes			
Knows how to read tables			
Shows confidence when reading new text			
Summarizes and synthesizes stories and informational texts			
Draws conclusions			
Makes inferences			
Knows how to read graphs			
Compares pieces of information presented visually			
Uses all available clues to make meaning			

Student Uses Strategy:
C = consistently S = sometimes R = rarely

Fluency Reading Strategy Checklist

	Reading Strategy Number and Card	Teacher Observations	Level	Student Uses Strategy...
CP 10	Preview the text before you read.	Student self-initiates text previewing.	M–P	
C8	Think about why a character is saying or doing something.	Student interprets traits and motivations.	I–P	
C9	Make sure you have questions in your mind before, during, and after reading.	Student asks him/herself questions while reading.	I–P	
C10	Think about the main idea of the book as you read.	Student identifies the main idea.	M–P	
C11	Think about the important details.	Student supports and separates details.	M–P	
C12	As you read, predict events and solutions to problems	Student creates and revises predictions.	M–P	
C13	You don't need to understand every word to understand the text.	Student reads for overall meaning, avoiding word-for word translation.	M–P	
C14	As you read, make judgments about what you read.	Student thinks critically	M–P	
C15	Make connections to your life, your other reading, and what you know.	Student connects text to self, text to text, and text to world.	M–P	
C16	Change your mind as you find new information in your reading	Student revises his or her thoughts and conclusions based on new information.	M–P	
C17	Think about what you need to remember as you continue to read.	Student sustains attention and memory over periods of time.	M–P	
C18	Make conclusions as you read.	Student draws conclusions.	M–T	
C19	As you read, summarize your reading in your head.	Student summarizes text (i.e., provides a short synopsis of reading).	Q–T	
C20	Use what you know to help you understand more than the words alone tell you.	Student makes inferences.	Q–T	

▶ **APPENDIX**

Reading Strategies

	Strategy in Student Language	Pedagogical Language	Levels	ELL Stages	Literacy Levels
CP1	Look at the pictures.	Student finds meaning with picture-text match.	A–B	1–5	E
CP2	Look at the words from left to right.	Student follows print left to right. *(Directionality of print)*	A–B	1–5	E
CP3	Point to each word as you read.	Student has one-to-one matching of voice to print/phonics clues.	A–B	1–5	E
CP4	When you get to the end of a line, go to the start of a new line.	Student uses return sweep.	A–B	1–5	E
CP5	Look for words you know.	Student recognizes high-frequency words.	A–H	3–5	E/Ea
CP6	Check for a pattern.	Student recognizes that there is a pattern to the text.	C–H	3–5	E/Ea
CP7	Does it sound right?	Student uses syntactic cues.	C–H	3	E/Ea
CP8	Think about the features, headings, bold print, charts, and diagrams.	Student looks at the features in a text to see what is important.	I–L	3–5	Ea/EF
CP9	Think about what you want to know to help you decide what part to read.	Student decides what part of the nonfiction text will provide the information needed.	I–L		Ea/EF
CP 10	Preview the text before you read.	Student self-initiates text-preview.	M–P		EF
C1	Use the pictures to help you understand the words.	Student reads a text using words and pictures.	A–B	1–5	E
C2	Think about what comes next and if it makes sense.	Student predicts what words or phrases will come next.	C–D	3–5	E/Ea
C3	Go back to the beginning of the paragraph and try again.	Student reads for deeper meaning in context.	I-L	3–5	Ea/EF
C4	Think about the elements of the story.	Student thinks about the elements of the story.	I–L	3–5	Ea/EF

KEY   E = Emergent   Ea = Early   EF = Early Fluent   F = Fluent

	Strategy in Student Language	Pedagogical Language	Levels	ELL Stages	Literacy Levels
C5	Ask yourself if what you are reading makes sense.	Student adjusts pace and monitors comprehension.	I–L	3–5	Ea/EF
C6	Predict what might happen next.	Student predicts what will happen.	I–L	3–5	Ea/EF
C7	Think about something you may have read or heard or done before.	Student uses previous experiences to help with understanding.	I–L	3–5	Ea/EF
C8	Think about why a character is saying or doing something.	Student interprets traits and motivations.	I–P	4–5	Ea/EF/F
C9	Have questions in your mind before, during, and after reading.	Student asks him/herself questions while reading.	I–P	4–5	EF/F
C10	Think about the main idea of the book as you read.	Student identifies the main idea.	M–P	3–5	EF/F
C11	Think about the important details.	Student supports and separates important details.	M–P	3–5	EF/F
C12	As you read, predict events and solutions to problems.	Student creates and revises predictions.	M–P	3–5	EF/F
C13	You don't need to understand every word to understand the text.	Student avoids word-for-word translation and adjusts pace.	M–P	3–5	EF/F
C14	As you read, make judgments about what you read.	Student thinks critically.	M–P	3–5	EF/F
C15	Make connections to your life, your other reading, and what you know.	Student connects text to self, text to text, and text to world.	M–P	3–5	EF/F
C16	Change your mind as you find new information in your reading.	Student revises thoughts and conclusions based on new information.	M–P	3–5	EF/F
C17	Think about what you need to remember as you continue to read this book.	Student sustains attention and memory over extended periods of time.	M–P	3–5	EF/F
C18	Make conclusions as you read.	Student draws conclusions.	M–T	3–5	EF/F
C19	As you read, summarize your reading in your head.	Student summarizes text.	Q–T	3–5	F
C20	Use what you know to help you understand more than the words alone tell you.	Student makes inferences.	Q–T	3–5	F

KEY E = Emergent   Ea = Early   EF = Early Fluent   F = Eluent

Reading and Language Characteristics

Level A

Reading Characteristics
- 20 to 25 words
- average sentence length: 3–6 words
- 1 patterned-language sentence with one word change per spread
- punctuation: period, question mark, exclamation point
- concepts familiar to children or grade-level content
- story line that focuses on a single idea
- realistic illustration or photographs
- precise text-picture match
- Fiction: Realistic Fiction introduced; Nonfiction: Expository, Personal Narrative introduced

Language Learning Characteristics
- natural language with controlled vocabulary based on 20 high-frequency words, grade-level content-area words, and grade K interest words*
- simple sentence structures: subject-verb, subject-verb-object-adverb or prepositional phrase
- focus on language useful for classroom learning and academic success
- literary grammatical structures that are difficult for language learners avoided (e.g., *Away went the lion.*)
- multicultural perspectives emphasized

Level B

Reading Characteristics
- 50 to 75 words
- average sentence length: 3–6 words or 8–10 words
- 1 or 2 patterned-language sentences with one word or phrase change
- concepts familiar to children or grade-level content
- punctuation: period, question mark, exclamation point, quotation marks, comma
- story line that focuses on a single idea
- return sweep introduced
- lines broken at natural phrasing
- realistic illustration or photographs
- precise text-picture match
- dialogue with speaker tags containing *said* and *asked* introduced
- Fiction: Animal Fantasy introduced

Language Learning Characteristics
- natural language with controlled vocabulary based on 40 high-frequency words, grade-level content-area words, and grade K interest words*
- sentence structures more complex, (e.g., subject-verb-object-prepositional phrase)
- focus on language useful for classroom learning and academic success
- literary grammatical structures that are difficult for language learners avoided (e.g., *Away went the lion.*)
- multicultural perspectives emphasized

Level C

Reading Characteristics
- 50 to 100 words
- average sentence length: 4 words
- as many as 3–4 sentence patterns in a text; not all sentences based on sentence patterns
- concepts familiar to children or grade-level content
- story line straightforward and requires little interpretation
- punctuation: period, question mark, exclamation point, quotation marks, comma
- lines broken at natural phrasing
- realistic illustration or photographs
- strong text-picture match
- dialogue of two speakers may appear on one page

Language Learning Characteristics
- natural language with controlled vocabulary based on 60 high-frequency words, grade-level content-area words, and late grade K interest words*
- emphasis on increased verb endings
- possessives introduced
- two-part verbs introduced (e.g., *call up*)
- infinitive construction and multiple prepositional phrases introduced
- focus on language useful for classroom learning and academic success
- literary grammatical structures that are difficult for language learners avoided
- multicultural perspectives emphasized

* interest word grade levels refer to on-grade-level reading vocabulary for native speakers

Level D

Reading Characteristics

- 90 to 140 words
- average sentence length: 5 words
- limited number of sentences based on sentence patterns
- story line with several episodes, possibly repetitive
- punctuation: period, question mark, exclamation point, quotation marks, comma
- dialogue of two named speakers with speaker tags *said* and *asked* appears on one page
- lines broken at natural phrasing
- realistic illustration or photographs
- strong text-picture match
- Informational Fiction introduced
- Nonfiction features: materials list introduced

Language Learning Characteristics

- natural language with controlled vocabulary based on 105 high-frequency words, grade-level content-area words, and early grade 1 interest words*
- compound words introduced
- contractions *I'm* and *it's* introduced
- words in a series introduced
- focus on language useful for classroom learning and academic success
- literary grammatical structures that are difficult for language learners avoided (e.g., *Away went the lion.*)
- multicultural perspectives emphasized

Level E

Reading Characteristics

- 100 to 175 words
- average sentence length: 6 words
- repetitive language based on phrases only
- concepts possibly new ideas related to familiar ones
- story line with several episodes, possibly repetitive
- characters' personalities developed
- dialogue of two named speakers with speaker tags *said* and *asked* appears on one page
- lines broken at natural phrasing
- realistic illustration or photographs
- strong text-picture match
- Fiction: Mystery and Play introduced; Nonfiction: Procedural introduced
- Nonfiction features: contents page, picture glossary, and recipe introduced

Language Learning Characteristics

- natural language with controlled vocabulary based on 105 high-frequency words, grade-level content-area words, and grade 1 interest words*
- compound words: possibly several in text
- two-part verbs emphasized (e.g., *call up*)
- compound sentences with *and* and *but* introduced
- multisyllabic words introduced but limited
- focus on language useful for classroom learning and academic success
- literary grammatical structures that are difficult for language learners avoided (e.g., *Away went the lion.*)
- multicultural perspectives emphasized

Level F

Reading Characteristics

- 125 to 200 words
- average sentence length: 7 words
- repetitive language based on phrases only if present
- story line with several episodes, possibly repetitive
- characters' personalities developed
- dialogue of multiple lines with speaker tags
- lines broken at natural phrasing
- paragraphs with extra spacing introduced
- realistic illustration or photographs
- strong text-picture match
- Nonfiction: Question and Answer and Picture Dictionary introduced
- Nonfiction features: maps with simple key and compass rose introduced

Language Learning Characteristics

- natural language and book language with controlled vocabulary based on 175 high-frequency words, grade-level content-area words, and grade 1 interest words*
- compound words: possibly multiple in text
- all common contractions allowed
- emphasis on adverbs and adverbial phrases
- prepositional phrases increasing in number and complexity
- adjective clauses with *who* and *where* as defining adjectives introduced
- compound sentences with *or* introduced
- multisyllabic words increasing
- focus on language useful for classroom learning and academic success
- literary grammatical structures that are difficult for language learners avoided (e.g., *Away went the lion.*)
- multicultural perspectives emphasized

interest word grade levels refer to on-grade-level reading vocabulary for native speakers

Level G

Reading Characteristics

- 150 to 225 words
- average sentence length: 8 words
- concepts more challenging; some technical words introduced in context
- story line includes a variety of characters
- interpretation of characters required
- dialogue's speaker tags sometimes embedded in larger sentences
- lines broken at natural phrasing
- abbreviations *Mr.* and *Mrs.* introduced
- realistic illustration or photographs
- supportive text-picture match
- Fiction: Humor introduced
- Nonfiction features: picture index introduced

Language Learning Characteristics

- natural language and book language with controlled vocabulary based on 175 high-frequency words, grade-level content-area words, and grade 1 interest words*
- compound words: used freely
- adjective clauses with *that* introduced
- compound sentences emphasized
- increasingly challenging verbs (*have to + verb, going to + verb*)
- multisyllabic words increasing
- focus on language useful for classroom learning and academic success
- literary grammatical structures that are difficult for language learners avoided (e.g., *Away went the lion.*)
- multicultural perspectives emphasized

Level H

Reading Characteristics

- 175 to 250 words
- average sentence length: 8 words
- concepts more challenging; technical words in context common
- interpretation of events required
- interpretation of characters required
- dialogue's speaker tags sometimes embedded in larger sentence
- lines broken at natural phrasing
- realistic illustration or photographs
- supportive text-picture match
- Nonfiction features: inset maps and maps with callouts introduced

Language Learning Characteristics

- natural language and book language with controlled vocabulary based on 325 high-frequency words, grade-level content-area words, and grade 1 interest words*
- gerunds introduced (e.g., *Grandma enjoys baking.*)
- sentences with participial phrases in the present introduced (e.g., *She came in the door, looking at Lupe.*)
- multisyllabic words common
- focus on language useful for classroom learning and academic success
- multicultural perspectives emphasized

Level I

Reading Characteristics

- 250 to 350 words
- average sentence length: 9 words
- concepts more challenging; technical words in context common
- story line based on one main problem and solution with multiple events to remember
- interpretation of characters and their change over time required
- dialogue sometimes interrupted by speaker tags
- lines broken at natural phrasing
- realistic illustration or photographs
- supportive text-picture match
- Nonfiction: Interview introduced
- Nonfiction features: headings, regular index, regular glossary, and bulleted/numbered lists introduced

Language Learning Characteristics

- natural language and book language with controlled vocabulary based on 325 high-frequency words, grade-level content-area words, and late grade 1 interest words*
- complex sentences with *when, where, as,* and *while* introduced
- appositives introduced
- sentence adverbials *of course* and *at last* introduced
- adjectival clauses with *-ing* verbs introduced (e.g., *boy sitting on a chair*)
- focus on language useful for classroom learning and academic success
- multicultural perspectives emphasized

Level J

Reading Characteristics

- 300 to 500 words
- average sentence length: 10 words
- abstract concepts and technical words in context common
- story lines with passage of time introduced
- interpretation of characters and their change over time required
- adult paragraphing (indents, no spacing) introduced

Language Learning Characteristics

- natural language and book language with vocabulary based on 325 high-frequency words, grade-level content-area words, and early grade 2 interest words*
- present perfect and past perfect verb tenses introduced
- emphasis on multiple adverbs and adjectives
- sentences with dependent clauses using *because* introduced
- conditional clauses with *if* introduced

* interest word grade levels refer to on-grade-level reading vocabulary for native speakers

Level J

- non-primary font introduced
- color behind text introduced
- supportive text-picture match
- Nonfiction features: captions and diagrams with call-outs introduced

- tag questions introduced (e.g., *isn't it?*)
- language of speculation introduced (e.g., *must have [been], could have [been], may have [been], might have [been]*)
- focus on language useful for classroom learning and academic success
- multicultural perspectives emphasized

Level K

Reading Characteristics

- 400 to 600 words
- average sentence length: 11 words
- abstract concepts and technical words in context and challenging vocabulary common
- variety of writing styles
- characters with different perspectives
- dialogue of several speakers on a single page (with or without speaker tags) introduced
- adult paragraphing in 50% of books; line breaks occcur at natural phrasing in 50% of books
- supportive text-picture match
- Nonfiction features: flow charts with labels introduced

Language Learning Characteristics

- natural language and book language with vocabulary based on 325 high-frequency words, grade-level content-area words, and grade 2 interest words*
- compound-complex sentences introduced
- sentences with *so* introduced
- complex sentences with multiple dependent clauses introduced
- focus on language useful for classroom learning and academic success
- multicultural perspectives emphasized

Level L

Reading Characteristics

- 600 to 700 words
- average sentence length: 11 words
- concepts possibly well outside child's experience
- variety of writing styles
- characters with different perspectives
- punctuation: single quotation marks introduced
- speaker tags with substitutions for the words *said* and *asked*
- adult paragraphing with indentation introduced
- less realistic illustration styles introduced
- text-picture match enhances text
- Fiction: Folktale introduced; Nonfiction: Biography and Journal/ Observation Log introduced
- Nonfiction features: horizontal time lines, bird's-eye view, and sentence-length captions introduced

Language Learning Characteristics

- natural language and book language with vocabulary based on 325 high-frequency words, grade-level content-area words, and grade 2 interest words*
- sentences with *either* and *neither* introduced
- sentences with multiple conditions introduced (e.g., *If... and..., then...; If... but..., then...*)
- complex sentences with multiple dependent clauses emphasized
- focus on language useful for classroom learning and academic success
- multicultural perspectives emphasized

Level M

Reading Characteristics

- 800 to 1000 words
- average sentence length: 12 words
- historical concepts introduced
- technical terms that are explained in context introduced
- punctuation: colon for lists introduced
- text-picture match that enhances text
- Fiction: Fantasy introduced; Nonfiction: Encyclopedia introduced
- Fiction features: e-mail and letters within text introduced
- Nonfiction features: size comparison diagrams, diagrams with labels, subheadings and simple sidebars introduced

Language Learning Characteristics

- natural language and book language with vocabulary based on 325 high-frequency words, grade-level content-area words, and grade 3 interest words*
- three-clause sentences emphasized
- prepositional phrases used in serial lists introduced
- passive voice with an agent is introduced but used sparingly
- initial *because* clauses are now common
- complex sentences with subordinate conjunctions *even though, whether,* and *unless*
- sentences with participial phrases in the past introduced (e.g., *He fell asleep, exhausted by the day's work.*)
- phrases combined with *then* (e.g., *He showered, then shaved and dressed.*)
- focus on language useful for classroom learning and academic success
- multicultural perspectives emphasized

* interest word grade levels refer to on-grade-level reading vocabulary for native speakers

Level N

Reading Characteristics
- 1400 to 1600 words for fiction
- 1100 to 1300 words for nonfiction
- average sentence length: 13 words
- concepts well outside child's experience
- characters that exhibit moral behavior, change during the story, and elicit sympathy emphasized
- suspense and irony introduced
- student needs to draw conclusions
- flashback and story within story introduced
- interpretation of illustration required
- introduction of italicized non-English terms whose meanings are derived from context (e.g., *Abuelito* Tito)
- Nonfiction features: sidebars with bulleted lists, tables with 2 rows, satellite images, and simple floor plans introduced

Language Learning Characteristics
- natural language and book language with vocabulary based on grade-level content area words and grade 3 interest words*
- adjective clauses common: defining clauses with *that*, non-defining clauses with *which*, and defining and non-defining clauses with *who*
- final ellipsis introduced (e.g., *Rachel is smarter than he [ellipses].*)
- passive voice without an agent introduced but used sparingly
- negative adverbs that negate a sentence without *no* or *not* introduced: (e.g., *barely, hardly, scarcely, rarely, seldom*)
- adjectival clauses with past participles introduced (e.g., *machine invented by a woman*)
- focus on language useful for classroom learning and academic success
- multicultural perspectives emphasized

Level O

Reading Characteristics
- 1700 to 1900 words for fiction
- 1400 to 1600 words for nonfiction
- average sentence length: 14 words
- detailed descriptions emphasized
- many opportunities for reader to use inference
- complicated issues introduced: war, death, freedom, justice
- chapter books introduced
- text-picture match that enhances text
- Nonfiction features: maps with complex compass rose, tables with 4 rows, and cross sections introduced

Language Learning Characteristics
- natural language and book language with vocabulary based on grade-level content area words and grade 3 interest words*
- variety of sentence adverbials introduced in initial position (e.g., <u>Honestly</u>, *we don't need any help.*)
- habitual past tense with *would* introduced
- sentences in parentheses introduced
- hyphenated adjectives with number introduced (e.g., *three-bedroom house*)
- clauses with subordinate conjunction *as if* introduced
- multiple-meaning words with two uses within text introduced
- focus on language useful for classroom learning and academic success
- multicultural perspectives emphasized

Level P

Reading Characteristics
- 2200 to 2400 words for fiction
- 1700 to 1900 words for nonfiction
- average sentence length: 15 words
- detailed descriptions of settings emphasized
- punctuation: colon and dash within sentence introduced
- text-picture match that extends text
- Fiction: Adventure introduced
- Nonfiction features: captions of several sentences that extend text, bar graphs, circle graphs, and simple flow charts with sentence-length captions introduced

Language Learning Characteristics
- natural language and book language with vocabulary based on grade-level content area words and grade 4 interest words*
- academic sentence adverbials *however* and *therefore* introduced
- passive voice common
- two-part verbs followed by prepositions introduced (e.g., *Call me up by Monday.*)
- ellipsis within a sentence introduced (e.g., *My camera, like Peter's [ellipses], is digital.*)
- infinitives phrases common
- focus on language useful for classroom learning and academic success
- multicultural perspectives emphasized

* interest word grade levels refer to on-grade-level reading vocabulary for native speakers

Level Q

Reading Characteristics
- 2500 to 2700 words for fiction
- 2000 to 2200 words for nonfiction
- average sentence length: 16 words
- mature themes such as prejudice introduced
- text-picture match that extends text
- Fiction: Science Fiction introduced; Blended Genres, such as Fantasy within Realistic Fiction and Mystery with Adventure, introduced
- Nonfiction features: maps with multiple-element keys, vertical time lines, captions with questions requiring picture interpretation

Language Learning Characteristics
- natural language and book language with vocabulary based on grade-level content area words and grade 4 interest words*
- multiple sentences with three clauses on a page
- parenthetical statements inside sentences introduced
- requests in declarative sentences (e.g., *I'd like to know your name.*)
- varying registers within text introduced
- focus on language useful for classroom learning and academic success
- literary grammatical structures allowed but controlled
- multicultural perspectives emphasized

Level R

Reading Characteristics
- 3000 to 3500 words for fiction
- 2200 to 2400 words for nonfiction
- average sentence length: 17 words
- simile and metaphor emphasized
- time and historical concepts emphasized
- multiple layers of meaning within text
- mature handling of issues such as death
- text-picture match that extends text
- Fiction: Diary introduced
- Nonfiction features: maps with scale, maps with change over time, parallel time lines, sidebars that extend text, scale diagrams, and line graphs introduced

Language Learning Characteristics
- natural language and book language with vocabulary based on grade-level content area words and grade 4 interest words*
- sentence adverbials within sentence introduced (e.g., *She does not, thankfully, know the truth.*)
- subjunctive mood introduced (e.g., *If I were a bird, I'd fly away. I demand that he tell me the truth.*)
- complex sentences with *for* and *yet* as coordinating conjunctions
- ellipsis in a sentence
- focus on language useful for classroom learning and academic success
- multicultural perspectives emphasized

Level S

Reading Characteristics
- 4000 to 4500 words for fiction
- 2500 to 3000 words for nonfiction
- average sentence length: 18 words
- complex paragraphs emphasized
- indirect speech emphasized
- text-picture match that extends text
- Fiction: Historical Fiction introduced
- Nonfiction features: complex floor plans (floor plan with key), comparative visual representations of information (e.g., circle graph and bar graph), and microscopic images introduced

Language Learning Characteristics
- natural language and book language with vocabulary based on grade-level content area words and grade 5 interest words*
- sentences with 4 clauses introduced
- four-element verb phrases common (e.g., *I may have been jogging last Tuesday*)
- complex sentences with *though*
- multiple-meaning words with two uses on same page introduced
- focus on language useful for classroom learning and academic success
- multicultural perspectives emphasized

Level T

Reading Characteristics
- 5000 to 6000 words for fiction
- 3000 to 3500 words for nonfiction
- average sentence length: 20 words
- symbolism introduced
- mixing dialogue and indirect speech introduced
- text-picture match that extends text
- Nonfiction: Persuasive introduced
- Nonfiction features: tables with two-row heads and subdivided columns, double-bar graphs, complex flow charts, and double-line graphs introduced

Language Learning Characteristics
- natural language and book language with vocabulary based on grade-level content area words and grade 5 interest words*
- ellipsis more common
- two sentence adverbials within one sentence
- negative statements with subject inversion introduced
- four-clause sentences common
- focus on language useful for classroom learning and academic success
- multicultural perspectives emphasized

* interest word grade levels refer to on-grade-level reading vocabulary for native speakers

High-Frequency Word List

The list is cumulative so that each level includes previously introduced words.

Level A

20 words

a	can	here	Mom	the
and	car	I	my	this
are	Dad	is	on	we
at	go	look	see	you

Level B

20 new words, 40 words

am	for	his	it	over
baby	get	home	many	red
big	had	how	me	said
do	her	in	mother	school

Level C

20 new words, 60 words

be	he	not	time	walk
come	help	play	to	where
dog	him	she	too	with
down	like	they	up	your

Level D–E

45 new words, 105 words

all	from	land	one	then
away	good	little	out	today
back	grow	make	park	two
ball	has	milk	put	very
but	have	need	so	want
came	house	no	some	was
children	I'm	now	teacher	went
day	into	of	that	what
did	it's	oh	them	will

Level F–G

70 new words, 175 words

after	book	can't	door	find
again	boy	cat	eat	first
an	bus	didn't	every	fish
ask	by	don't	feet	got

70 new words, 175 words

just	Mrs.	please	sleep	their	were
know	Mr.	ran	something	there	who
live	new	read	still	thing	woman
long	next	right	stop	think	work
made	old	room	take	thought	yes
man	or	same	talk	took	
miss	other	saw	tell	us	
more	people	shout	thank	way	
morning	pet	sit	that's	well	

150 new words, 325 words

about	black	fast	jump	own	stay
across	blue	father	knew	paper	sun
add	boat	fell	last	past	than
again	bring	fire	laugh	pick	these
air	brother	five	left	place	those
almost	brown	food	let	pretty	three
along	call	found	let's	pull	together
also	care	four	lost	ready	told
always	catch	friend	lot	ride	top
animal	city	fun	love	river	tree
another	clean	gave	may	road	turn
any	close	girl	maybe	round	under
anything	cold	give	might	run	use
around	couldn't	green	money	sat	wasn't
as	cut	ground	move	say	watch
ate	does	hand	much	set	water
bad	done	happy	must	should	week
beautiful	each	hard	name	show	when
before	easy	head	never	sister	which
began	end	hill	night	six	while
begin	enough	hold	once	small	white
behind	everyone	I'll	only	someone	why
best	everything	I've	open	sometimes	without
better	fall	inside	our	soon	year
between	farm	isn't	outside	start	yellow

InStep Readers Scope and Sequence

Reading Strategies

Concepts of Print		
Find meaning with picture-text match	**A–B**
Follow print from left to right (directionality of print)	**A–B**
One-to-one matching of voice to print and phonics clues	**A–B**
Use return sweep	**A–B**
Recognize high-frequency words	**A–H**
Recognize that there is a pattern to the text	**C–H**
Use syntactic cues	**C–H**
Look at the features in a nonfiction text to help figure out what is important	**I–L**
Decide what part of the nonfiction text will provide the information needed	**I–L**
Self-initiate text previewing	**M–P**

Comprehension		
Read a text using words and pictures	**A–B**
Predict what words or phrases will come next	**C–H**
Read for deeper meaning in context	**I–L**
Think about the elements of the story	**I–L**
Adjust pace and monitor comprehension	**I–L**
Predict what is going to happen	**I–L**
Use previous experiences to help with understanding	**I–L**
Interpret traits and motivations	**I–P**
Ask questions while reading	**I–P**
Identify the main idea	**M–P**
Support and separate important details	**M–P**
Create and revise predictions	**M–P**
Read for overall meaning, avoiding word-for-word translation, and adjust pace while reading	**M–P**
Think critically	**M–P**
Connect text to self, text to text, and text to world	**M–P**
Revise thoughts and conclusions based on new information	**M–P**
Sustain attention and memory over extended periods of time in longer reading	**M–P**

Draw conclusions	**M–T**	
Summarize text, i.e., provide a short synopsis of reading	**Q–T**	
Make inferences	**Q–T**	

Reading Skills

Comprehension	Read dialogue with speaker tags	**B**
	Identify sentence patterns	**A B C**
	Read dialogue of two speakers	**C**
	Understand story line with several events	**D E**
	Recognize character traits	**E F**
	Use photographs during reading	**E**
	Analyze repetitive story events	**F**
	Understand dialogue of several lines	**F**
	Read paragraphs with extra spacing	**F**
	Recognize multiple characters	**G**
	Identify speaker tags embedded in larger sentence	**G H**
	Recognize abbreviations *Mr.* and *Mrs.*	**G**
	Understand technical words in context	**G H I K M**
	Interpret events	**H**
	Read speaker tags within dialogue	**H**
	Analyze story line with several events	**I**
	Read dialogue interrupted by speaker tags	**I**
	Analyze characters	**J K L**
	Understand passage of time	**J**
	Read dialogue between two speakers	**K**
	Read dialogue with expression	**L**
	Understand characters' perspectives	**L**
	Identify historical concepts	**M**
	Draw conclusions	**N**
	Make inferences	**O**

Understand detailed descriptions		O P
Read chapter books		O
Understand sophisticated themes		Q R
Understand simile and metaphor		R
Analyze meaning within text		R
Understand indirect speech		S
Identify symbolism		T
Understand dialogue and indirect speech		T

Punctuation	Recognize period	A B C
	Recognize question mark	A B
	Recognize exclamation point	A C
	Match text to pictures	A B C D Q T
	Recognize quotation marks	B C
	Use single quotation marks	L
	Use colon before a list	M
	Recognize colon and dash	P

Genre–Fiction	Realistic fiction genre	A B C J K S
	Animal fantasy genre	B D I
	Informational fiction genre	D J
	Play genre	E F H K
	Mystery Genre	E N
	Humor genre	G J
	Folktale genre	L N
	Fantasy genre	M P
	Adventure genre	P
	Science fiction genre	Q
	Blended genres	Q
	Diary genre	R
	Historical fiction genre	S

Genre–Nonfiction	Expository genre	A B C D E K L N Q S
	Personal narrative genre	A C D
	Procedural genre	E J N
	Picture dictionary genre	F J
	Question-and-answer genre	F Q S
	Interview genre	K
	Biography genre	L N
	Journal/observation log genre	L
	Encyclopedia genre	M
	Persuasive genre	T
Nonfiction Features	Materials list	D G K
	Table of contents page	E F K
	Picture glossary	E G
	Map with simple compass rose	F
	Recipe (procedural text)	E G J
	Picture index	G H
	Inset map	H I
	Map with call-outs	H
	Bulleted list	I
	Index	I
	Headings	I K
	Captions	J
	Diagram with call-outs	J
	Glossary	K
	Sentence-length captions	L P
	Time line	L O P Q
	E-mail within text	M
	Subheadings	M N
	Scale diagram	M R
	Sidebars	M R

Nonfiction Features		
Floor plan	N	
Table with two rows	N	
Four-row table	O	
Complex compass rose	O	
Cross section	O	
Flow chart	P	
Bar graph	P	S
Circle graph	P	
Captions with questions	Q	
Map with mulitple-element key	Q	
Map with scale	R	
Map with change over time	R	
Line graph	R	S
Parallel time line	R	
Complex floor plan	S	
Microscopic images	S	
Double-bar graph and double-line graph	T	
Complex flow chart	T	
Two-column table	T	

Developmental Phonics

Phonemic Awareness			
Sound matching	A		
Phoneme blending	A	B	C
Word awareness	A	B	C
Syllable awareness	A	B	C
Sound isolation	A	B	C
Rhyming words	B	C	
Adding sounds	D	E	
Deleting sounds	E		

Phonics		
Initial consonants	A	
Short-vowel word families	B D	
Long-vowel CVCe word families	D E	
Consonant blends and digraphs	F G	
Word families with vowel digraphs	H	
Long-vowel word families	H	
Final blends	I	
Consonant patterns	J	
r-Controlled word families	K	
Word families with diphthongs	K	
Vowel patterns	L	
Consonant patterns	M	

Word Study		
Adjectives	N	
Verbs	N	
Prepositions	N	
Prefixes	N O P Q	
Contractions	N S	
Multiple-meaning words	O Q S	
Adverbs	O	
Nouns	O	
Consonant doubling	O S	
Suffixes	P Q T	
Pronouns	P	
Conjunctions	P	
Connotation vs. denotation	Q T	
Analogies	Q T	
Cognates	R	
Abbreviations	R S	
Antonyms	R	
Open and closed syllables	R	

Inflected endings	**R**
Compound words	**S**
Homonyms	**T**

Language Skills

Identify parts of a sentence	**A B**
Recognize high-frequency words	**A B**
Recognize possessives	**C**
Understand prepositional phrases	**C F**
Recognize verb endings	**C**
Use infinitives	**C P**
Use two-part verbs	**C E**
Identify contractions	**D F**
Recognize words in a series	**D**
Identify compound words	**D E F G**
Read compound sentences with *and* and *but*	**E**
Understand *who* and *where* clauses	**F**
Identify adverbs	**F O R**
Read compound sentences with *or*	**F**
Understand verbs *going to* and *have to*	**G**
Read compound sentences	**G**
Understand multi-syllabic words	**G H**
Understand *that* clauses	**G**
Use gerunds	**H**
Identify phrases with *-ing*	**H**
Understand *when, where, as,* and *while* clauses	**I**
Identify appositives	**I**
Understand adjective clauses with *-ing*	**I**
Understand *of course* and *at last*	**I**
Identify tag questions	**J**

Identify present perfect and past perfect verbs	**J**
Identify multiple adjectives and adverbs	**J T**
Understand verb *must have been*	**J**
Understand *because* and *if* clauses	**J**
Read sentences with *so*	**K**
Read compound-complex sentences	**K**
Read complex sentences	**K**
Use multiple dependent clauses	**K**
Understand sentences with *either* and *neither*	**L**
Understand sentences with *If . . . then . . .*	**L**
Read complex sentences with multiple dependent clauses	**L**
Understand phrases with *-ed*	**M**
Recognize phrases with *then*	**M**
Understand *because* clauses	**M**
Read three-clause sentences	**M Q**
Understand *even though, whether,* and *unless* clauses	**M**
Read prepositional phrases used in a list	**M**
Use passive verbs	**M P**
Understand adjective clauses with *-ed*	**N**
Identify adverbs *hardly* and *barely*	**N**
Recognize passive voice	**N P**
Understand *that, which,* and *who* clauses	**N**
Identify ellipsis	**N R**
Understand past tense with *would*	**O**
Identify adjectives with hyphens	**O**
Understand *as if* clauses	**O**
Recognize sentences in parentheses	**O**
Understand multiple-meaning words	**O S**
Use two-part verbs + prepositions	**P**
Identify ellipses within a sentence	**P T**
Use infinitives	**P**
Understand adverbs *however* and *therefore*	**P**

Recognize requests	**Q**
Use formal and informal language	**Q**
Recognize literary language	**Q**
Understand parentheses inside sentences	**Q**
Recognize subjunctive	**R**
Read compound sentences with *yet* and *for*	**R**
Understand *Though* clauses	**S**
Read four-clause sentences	**T**
Understand negative statements	**T**

Fluency

Use punctuation when reading aloud	**A–I**
Stress words in bold and italics when reading aloud	**D–I**
Change your voice for different characters when reading aloud	**J–M**
Read aloud with appropriate phrasing	**J–T**
Change your voice to show characters' feelings	**N–T**

Leveling Correlations

InStep Readers Rigby ELL Levels	Fountas and Pinnell Level	*Rigby READS* Instructional or Independent Reading Level	Developmental Reading Assessment (DRA) Level	Early Intervention Level (EIL) Reading Recovery	Basal Reading Level
A	A	Early Readiness	A–1	1	K (Readiness)
B	B	Kindergarten	2	2	K (Readiness)
C	C	1–1	3	3–4	Grade 1 (Pre-Primer)
D	D	1–2	4	5–6	Grade 1 (Pre-Primer)
E	E	1–3	6–8	7–8	Grade 1 (Pre-Primer)
F	F	1–4	10	9–10	Grade 1
G	G	1–5	12	11–12	Grade 1
H	H	1–6	14	13–14	Grade 1
I	I	1–7	16	15–16	Grade 1
J	J	2–1	18	17–18	Grade 2
K	K	2–2	20	19–20	Grade 2
L	L	2–3	24		Grade 2
M	M	2–4	28		Grade 2
N	N	3–1	30		Grade 3
O	O	3–2	34		Grade 3
P	P	3–3	38		Grade 3
Q	Q	4–1	40		Grade 4
R	R	4–2	40		Grade 4
S	S	4–3	40		Grade 4
T	T	5–1	44		Grade 5

Levels are subjective. Adjust designated levels according to your personal evaluation.